PERSONAL DETAILS

Y0-CUZ-236

name:
passport number:
nationality:
birthdate:
home address:

mobile telephone:
home telephone:
email address:

hair color:
eye color:
height:
weight:
blood type:
allergies:

emergency contact:
emergency telephone:

medical contact:
medical telephone:

IMPORTANT CONTACT INFORMATION

insurance company:
insurance telephone:
insurance address:

airline:
airline telephone:

accomodation:
accomodation contact:
acommodation telephone:
accomodation:
accomodation contact:
accomodation telephone:

bank:
bank telephone:
bank location:

bank:
bank telephone:
bank location:

other information:

THINGS TO PACK

- ○ ADAPTERS
- ○ AIRLINE TICKETS
- ○ BATTERIES
- ○ BOOKS TO READ
- ○ CAMERA
- ○ CAMERA BATTERY CHARGER
- ○ CAMERA FLASH CARD
- ○ CELL PHONE
- ○ CELL PHONE CHARGER
- ○ CONTACT LENSES
- ○ CREDIT CARDS
- ○ DRIVER'S LICENSE
- ○ GUIDE BOOKS
- ○ HAIR DRYER
- ○ HAT / GLOVES
- ○ INSURANCE PAPERS
- ○ IPOD
- ○ JEWELRY / WATCH
- ○ LAPTOP
- ○ LAPTOP CHARGER
- ○ MEDICINE
- ● JOURNAL
- ○ PASSPORT
- ○ READING GLASSES
- ○ SNACKS
- ○ SUNGLASSES
- ○ TOILETRIES
- ○ TOWEL
- ○ UMBRELLA
- ○ WALKING SHOES
- ○ WATER BOTTLE

ITINERARY

date:
leave for airport by:
depart from:
flight number:
departure time:
destination:
arrival time:
taxi telephone:
notes:

date:
leave for airport by:
depart from:
flight number:
departure time:
destination:
arrival time:
taxi telephone:
notes:

ITINERARY

date:
leave for airport by:
depart from:
flight number:
departure time:
destination:
arrival time:
taxi telephone:
notes:

date:
leave for airport by:
depart from:
flight number:
departure time:
destination:
arrival time:
taxi telephone:
notes:

ITINERARY

date:
leave for airport by:
depart from:
flight number:
departure time:
destination:
arrival time:
taxi telephone:
notes:

date:
leave for airport by:
depart from:
flight number:
departure time:
destination:
arrival time:
taxi telephone:
notes:

ITINERARY

date:
leave for airport by:
depart from:
flight number:
departure time:
destination:
arrival time:
taxi telephone:
notes:

date:
leave for airport by:
depart from:
flight number:
departure time:
destination:
arrival time:
taxi telephone:
notes:

ACCOMODATION

name:
city:
address:
telephone number:
resident contact:
cost:
duration / nights:
check in time:
check out time:
notes:

name:
city:
address:
telephone number:
resident contact:
cost:
duration / nights:
check in time:
check out time:
notes:

ACCOMODATION

name:
city:
address:
telephone number:
resident contact:
cost:
duration / nights:
check in time:
check out time:
notes:

name:
city:
address:
telephone number:
resident contact:
cost:
duration / nights:
check in time:
check out time:
notes:

ACCOMODATION

name:
city:
address:
telephone number:
resident contact:
cost:
duration / nights:
check in time:
check out time:
notes:

name:
city:
address:
telephone number:
resident contact:
cost:
duration / nights:
check in time:
check out time:
notes:

ACCOMODATION

name:
city:
address:
telephone number:
resident contact:
cost:
duration / nights:
check in time:
check out time:
notes:

name:
city:
address:
telephone number:
resident contact:
cost:
duration / nights:
check in time:
check out time:
notes:

ACCOMODATION

name:
city:
address:
telephone number:
resident contact:
cost:
duration / nights:
check in time:
check out time:
notes:

name:
city:
address:
telephone number:
resident contact:
cost:
duration / nights:
check in time:
check out time:
notes:

ACCOMODATION

name:
city:
address:
telephone number:
resident contact:
cost:
duration / nights:
check in time:
check out time:
notes:

name:
city:
address:
telephone number:
resident contact:
cost:
duration / nights:
check in time:
check out time:
notes:

PEOPLE I'VE MET ALONG THE WAY

name:
where we met:
email address:
telephone number:
mailing address:

their story:

name:
where we met:
email address:
telephone number:
mailing address:

their story:

PEOPLE I'VE MET ALONG THE WAY

name:
where we met:
email address:
telephone number:
mailing address:

their story:

name:
where we met:
email address:
telephone number:
mailing address:

their story:

PEOPLE I'VE MET ALONG THE WAY

name:
where we met:
email address:
telephone number:
mailing address:

their story:

name:
where we met:
email address:
telephone number:
mailing address:

their story:

PEOPLE I'VE MET ALONG THE WAY

name:
where we met:
email address:
telephone number:
mailing address:

their story:

name:
where we met:
email address:
telephone number:
mailing address:

their story:

PEOPLE I'VE MET ALONG THE WAY

name:
where we met:
email address:
telephone number:
mailing address:

their story:

name:
where we met:
email address:
telephone number:
mailing address:

their story:

PEOPLE I'VE MET ALONG THE WAY

name:
where we met:
email address:
telephone number:
mailing address:

their story:

name:
where we met:
email address:
telephone number:
mailing address:

their story:

JOURNAL ENTRIES

day: date: | |
location:
weather: ◯ sunny   ◯ cloudy   ◯ rainy   ◯ snowy   ◯ windy
today's plans:

how the story will be told:

JOURNAL ENTRIES

websites and addresses of places to remember:

JOURNAL ENTRIES

day: date: | |
location:
weather: ◯ sunny   ◯ cloudy   ◯ rainy   ◯ snowy   ◯ windy
today's plans:

how the story will be told:

JOURNAL ENTRIES

websites and addresses of places to remember:

JOURNAL ENTRIES

day: date: | |
location:
weather: ☐ sunny   ☐ cloudy   ☐ rainy   ☐ snowy   ☐ windy
today's plans:

how the story will be told:

JOURNAL ENTRIES

websites and addresses of places to remember:

JOURNAL ENTRIES

day: date: | |
location:
weather: ○ sunny   ○ cloudy   ○ rainy   ○ snowy   ○ windy
today's plans:

how the story will be told:

JOURNAL ENTRIES

websites and addresses of places to remember:

JOURNAL ENTRIES

day: date: | |
location:
weather: ◯ sunny   ◯ cloudy   ◯ rainy   ◯ snowy   ◯ windy
today's plans:

how the story will be told:

JOURNAL ENTRIES

websites and addresses of places to remember:

JOURNAL ENTRIES

day: date: | |
location:
weather: ◯ sunny ◯ cloudy ◯ rainy ◯ snowy ◯ windy
today's plans:

how the story will be told:

JOURNAL ENTRIES

websites and addresses of places to remember:

JOURNAL ENTRIES

day: date: | |
location:
weather: ◯ sunny   ◯ cloudy   ◯ rainy   ◯ snowy   ◯ windy
today's plans:

how the story will be told:

JOURNAL ENTRIES

websites and addresses of places to remember:

JOURNAL ENTRIES

day: date: | |
location:
weather: ☐ sunny   ☐ cloudy   ☐ rainy   ☐ snowy   ☐ windy
today's plans:

how the story will be told:

JOURNAL ENTRIES

websites and addresses of places to remember:

JOURNAL ENTRIES

day: date:

location:

weather: ◯ sunny ◯ cloudy ◯ rainy ◯ snowy ◯ windy

today's plans:

how the story will be told:

JOURNAL ENTRIES

websites and addresses of places to remember:

JOURNAL ENTRIES

day:　　　　　　　　　date:　　|　　　|
location:
weather: ☐ sunny　☐ cloudy　☐ rainy　☐ snowy　☐ windy
today's plans:

how the story will be told:

JOURNAL ENTRIES

websites and addresses of places to remember:

JOURNAL ENTRIES

day: date: | |
location:
weather: ◯ sunny   ◯ cloudy   ◯ rainy   ◯ snowy   ◯ windy
today's plans:

how the story will be told:

JOURNAL ENTRIES

websites and addresses of places to remember:

JOURNAL ENTRIES

day: date: | |
location:
weather: ◯ sunny   ◯ cloudy   ◯ rainy   ◯ snowy   ◯ windy
today's plans:

how the story will be told:

JOURNAL ENTRIES

websites and addresses of places to remember:

JOURNAL ENTRIES

day: date:

location:

weather: ◯ sunny ◯ cloudy ◯ rainy ◯ snowy ◯ windy

today's plans:

how the story will be told:

JOURNAL ENTRIES

websites and addresses of places to remember:

JOURNAL ENTRIES

day: date: | |
location:
weather: ◯ sunny   ◯ cloudy   ◯ rainy   ◯ snowy   ◯ windy
today's plans:

how the story will be told:

JOURNAL ENTRIES

websites and addresses of places to remember:

JOURNAL ENTRIES

day:　　　　　　　　　date:　　|　　　|
location:
weather: ◯ sunny　◯ cloudy　◯ rainy　◯ snowy　◯ windy
today's plans:

how the story will be told:

JOURNAL ENTRIES

websites and addresses of places to remember:

JOURNAL ENTRIES

day:　　　　　　　　　date:　　|　　　|
location:
weather: ☐ sunny　☐ cloudy　☐ rainy　☐ snowy　☐ windy
today's plans:

how the story will be told:

JOURNAL ENTRIES

websites and addresses of places to remember:

JOURNAL ENTRIES

day:　　　　　　　　　date:　　　|　　　|
location:
weather: ◯ sunny　◯ cloudy　◯ rainy　◯ snowy　◯ windy
today's plans:

how the story will be told:

JOURNAL ENTRIES

websites and addresses of places to remember:

JOURNAL ENTRIES

day:　　　　　　　　date:　　　|　　　　|
location:
weather: ◯ sunny　◯ cloudy　◯ rainy　◯ snowy　◯ windy
today's plans:

how the story will be told:

JOURNAL ENTRIES

websites and addresses of places to remember:

JOURNAL ENTRIES

day:　　　　　　　　date:　　　|　　　　|
location:
weather: ○ sunny　○ cloudy　○ rainy　○ snowy　○ windy
today's plans:

how the story will be told:

JOURNAL ENTRIES

websites and addresses of places to remember:

JOURNAL ENTRIES

day:　　　　　　　　　date:　　|　　　|
location:
weather: ○ sunny　○ cloudy　○ rainy　○ snowy　○ windy
today's plans:

how the story will be told:

JOURNAL ENTRIES

websites and addresses of places to remember:

JOURNAL ENTRIES

day: date: | |
location:
weather: ◯ sunny   ◯ cloudy   ◯ rainy   ◯ snowy   ◯ windy
today's plans:

how the story will be told:

JOURNAL ENTRIES

websites and addresses of places to remember:

JOURNAL ENTRIES

day: date:

location:
weather: ☐ sunny   ☐ cloudy   ☐ rainy   ☐ snowy   ☐ windy
today's plans:

how the story will be told:

JOURNAL ENTRIES

websites and addresses of places to remember:

SEND POSTCARDS

name:
telephone:
email:
mailing address:

name:
telephone:
email:
mailing address:

name:
telephone:
email:
mailing address:

name:
telephone:
email:
mailing address:

SEND POSTACARDS

name:
telephone:
email:
mailing address:

name:
telephone:
email:
mailing address:

name:
telephone:
email:
mailing address:

name:
telephone:
email:
mailing address:

SEND POSTACARDS

name:
telephone:
email:
mailing address:

name:
telephone:
email:
mailing address:

name:
telephone:
email:
mailing address:

name:
telephone:
email:
mailing address:

SEND POSTACARDS

name:
telephone:
email:
mailing address:

name:
telephone:
email:
mailing address:

name:
telephone:
email:
mailing address:

name:
telephone:
email:
mailing address:

PEOPLE TO SHOP FOR

name:
telephone:
email:
stuff they like:

what i bought:

name:
telephone:
email:
stuff they like:

what i bought:

PEOPLE TO SHOP FOR

name:
telephone:
email:
stuff they like:

what i bought:

name:
telephone:
email:
stuff they like:

what i bought:

PEOPLE TO SHOP FOR

name:
telephone:
email:
stuff they like:

what i bought:

name:
telephone:
email:
stuff they like:

what i bought:

PEOPLE TO SHOP FOR

name:
telephone:
email:
stuff they like:

what i bought:

name:
telephone:
email:
stuff they like:

what i bought:

MEMOIRS

MEMOIRS

MEMOIRS

MEMOIRS

MEMOIRS

MEMOIRS

MEMOIRS

MEMOIRS

MEMOIRS

MEMOIRS

MEMOIRS

MEMOIRS

MEMOIRS

MEMOIRS

MEMOIRS

MEMOIRS

MEMOIRS

MEMOIRS

MEMOIRS

MEMOIRS

MEMOIRS

MEMOIRS

MEMOIRS

MEMOIRS

MEMOIRS

TRIM ABOVE THIS LINE AND GLUE ALONG THE EDGES
ON THE FOLLOWING PAGE TO CREATE A POCKET

POCKET FOR TICKET STUBS AND RECEIPTS

GLUE GENTLY ALONG THE GREY EDGES
AND CLOSE THE PAGES TOGETHER
TO MAKE A DO IT YOURSELF POCKET.

IT IS GOOD FOR FLAT PAPER ITEMS
INCLUDING STUBS AND RECEIPTS

GLUE GENTLY ALONG THE GREY EDGES
AND CLOSE THE PAGES TOGETHER
TO MAKE A DO IT YOURSELF POCKET.

IT IS GOOD FOR FLAT PAPER ITEMS
INCLUDING STUBS AND RECEIPTS

ENJOY YOUR TRIP
KEEP ALERT AND STAY SAFE!

THANK YOU FOR TAKING US ALONG FOR THE RIDE!

FIND THIS TRAVEL GUIDE ON AMAZON
BY AUTHOR JOE DOLAN

Made in the USA
San Bernardino, CA
30 October 2017